Homegrown

Homegrown
Poems by
Christine Coates

Published in 2014 by Modjaji Books
PO Box 385, Athlone, 7760, Cape Town, South Africa
www.modjajibooks.co.za

© Christine Coates
Christine Coates has asserted her right to be
identified as the author of this work.

All rights reserved.
No part of this book may be reproduced or transmitted in any
form or by any means, mechanical or electronic, including
photocopying or recording, or be stored in any information storage or retrieval system without permission from the
publisher.

ISBN 978-1-920590-81-9

Cover artwork by Christine Coates
Author photograph: Frenske Otzen
Book and cover layout by Danielle Clough
Edited by Joan Metelerkamp
Printed and bound by Megadigital, Cape Town

For my family

Contents

Old Roads	9
Circles	10
Kitchen stories	11
Homegrown	12
Home Times	14
School mornings before a test	15
Dust Music	16
Marguerites	18
The Sounds of School	19
The Girl from Qumbu	20
Tsitsa Falls	21
The day I wore yellow	22
The day she died	23
Papa	26
A Diet of Worms	27
Sterkfontein Bones	28
Sabotage	29
questions of the night	30
Nefertiti Round	**31**
poem for a blue crown	32
Red Poem	33
Museum in Berlin	34
poem for a white girl	35
Desert Heart	36
poem for a blue mother	37
Kalahari heart	38

Why we need darkness	40
Ash of Fire	41
After the Fires	42
Old Year	43
Morning Gifts	46
La Bourdique	47
Hiding like a Huguenot	48
Four Voices of Marriage	49
Maps of Memory	50
Marriage	51
hoping for birds	54
The story of how I love a river	55
Old Photographs in a Junk Shop	56
the Longitude of Water	58
equinox caller	59
found poem	60
the bush at sunrise	61
South Easter	62
red dress	63
on hearing my friend is to emigrate	64
myth of myself	66
Remembering Promises	67
House at Kolmanskop	68
Zwaanswyk Morning	69

Old Roads

The road out of Klerksdorp
is a hard road.
The road to Potch, to Jo'burg –
people get killed.
There was a smashed-up car
on top of a building,
and an aeroplane
on the roof of a petrol station.
I don't think that one was an accident
but as a child I did.

The road to Braamfontein –
where I studied the city's history
to teach to children –
I never found out who this Braam was,
and the other Bram, no one spoke of him;
I just taught the syllabus,
the names of roads –
Barry Herzog, Jan Smuts, D.F. Malan
and Hendrik Verwoerd.

Robben Island was a land beyond the sea.

Circles

In the early days a passport photo
was the only one I had;
in a circle of brass – it both took me away
and brought me back.
I think of conception, how I was born –
the circles of my mother's breasts
a universe of milk, first imprints –
her blue eyes.
Then I was a voyager in space; I wanted
to climb onto his shoulders, wanted
to hear, at the hour, his voice,
to twirl the hair on his chest.
My world began to expand before
it collapsed.
Now I long to feel the heat,
hear the fly screen door,
smell the roast lamb,
the mint being chopped,
the Sunday that
begins it all again.

Kitchen stories

In the breakfast newspaper
is a photograph – A Big Catch.
The fisherman had a lucky corner;
he was old – maybe a hundred.
He says we can all begin again.

I grew up on kitchen stories,
grandmother kneading dough
grandfather mending, by moonlight, his gun.
He wears his face like blank feathers,
night is in his throat.

Breakfast fables and tea;
children told to be mothers,
hinterland and concentration camp.
My khaki father, his desert glance,
tells me of an Englishman's war.

I hear the kitchen ghosts;
looking inside my gloves and shoes
I see someone composed of my pieces
allowing the day to act.

The voices of my children
call in the distance.
My son is a rooster foot,
behind the moon,
my daughter – a fish.

I tell my husband
I'm not your wife anymore
the distributor of happiness.
Like Cain, nomad collecting stones,
I'm making irredeemable
plans for my flesh.

Homegrown

Klerksdorp is still a dusty town
there the mine dumps blow dirt so fine
it mixes in one's cough, colours the blue gums
on the bordering ditches.

We lived there just beyond
where koppies and kameeldorings stretched
towards nowhere and ant heaps grew
to a man's knee, wild rabbits ran
to their burrows before the dogs
caught them.

We grew there near the mining slimes and
the mielie lands, where mineheads
stood sentry like our fathers
and the dominee.
Mother tried to tame the garden;
serpentine walls, rose gardens, sprinklers
to keep the brown at bay.

Papa subscribed there
to The Canadian Hunter
with photographs of foreign forests,
fish and lakes, while the dust caked
our furniture and, in winter,
frost blackened the camellias,
knocking pink buds
to the icy pathway.

Thunderstorms broke there –
soundless afternoons when my parents slept
after Sunday lunch, snakes hid in the shed
near the swing where we played;
if we shouted and woke Papa
he belted us.
One night my sister screamed;
her gown had caught fire

and, in the rising flames,
our father rushed her into the passage,
rolled her up like a sausage in the long runner.
Her eyes were saucers,
round and round.

I dreamed the house there
was set on fire by a wolf;
he threw my doll up into the flames
as he danced and laughed
on the end of the roof.

Home Times

The car's headlights cutting like a butcher's knife
into the yellow fat of meat
shiny and wet in the middle.
The flanks of beef and kudu hanging in the garage
waiting for my father to make biltong.
And guns – the gleaming metal, the sound of the bolt being pulled back,
the smell of the oil, the softness of the cloth to buff it,
guns used for clay pigeons, or the pellet guns
we aimed at bottles on a wall.

It is 1965 and I am in the back of a car driving along a dusty road
in the bushveld. My father is behind the wheel, my arms around his neck,
the canvas bag hanging from the front of his car as it speeds along,
hot dry days just to drink that cold water
and dark nights, the headlights searching for a signpost, or to stop for a rest
to drink hot tea from a flask, to dip rusks,
watch birds through his binoculars, the brown leather case they come in,
the smell of it, his Leica and its lens that concertinas out,
the taste of leather, the feel of it against my skin,
the fur of jackals sewn together in rows, tails dangling;
it was his kaross, my fingers where the eyes and ears had been.

The oily smell of the bush in the evening – I thought it was castor oil,
but it was the potato bush – when the sun is setting,
driving into the dark with a spotlight searching for bright eyes –
impala or the eyes of bush-babies jumping in the trees.
Campfires and log fires, him standing there
drinking beer from a bottle,
seeing him through the smoke,
the smell of Peter Stuyvesant,
the red glow of the tip through the night.

School mornings before a test

Footsteps of the milkman,
the clink of bottles –
I'm up early to study;
it's cold here in the Western Transvaal,
the light a dirty grey,
the unlikely hum of the milk cart,
its battery engine
down the street –
milk and orange juice.
Cars start up – dads taking kids to school,
maids walk from the bus stop
calling to one another
as they peel off into
individual driveways.

Dust Music

A bony woman,
she'd listen for a flat note
on the highveld, among mine heads,
teaching us songs from other lands.
On hot Transvaal afternoons
German folk songs, Italian love songs –
I love to go a-wandering –
in the dusty mining town in Africa.

Marguerites

I come from a long line of Margarets;
there was Granny Daisy Burl –
a Margaret who had a trading station
in the Transkei. She looked out of her window
into the eyes of a brown
Nguni cow.

And her mother Maggie Ala McGeoch
who sailed from Scotland and met
the young James McLellan.
All she had was her sewing machine;
they married.
Her mother, Margaret Gardner
lived in a castle without a roof,
She married McGeoch in Glasgow,
he owned the village
before the collapse of the bank, so
they packed for P.E. –
she took the family china.

And my own mother
Margaret McLellan Burl –
a name like spring daisies
strung on a necklace.

The Sounds of School

Umtata Station –
a hiss of steam, the scream of steel –
her trunk, her tuck box,
tennis rackets, hockey sticks, hankies and photo frames
a cabin of old girls, new girls,
the girl from Qumbu,
her two brothers and their stories of boarding school.

Boiling cabbage, spirogyra and frog's eggs,
half-term, mid-term;
all these are the senses of school –

and then the bugle call –

the caterpillar tracks, the clunking factories, coal fires,
the roar of the forties,
rumours, threats,
Hitler and Sieg Heil,

The bugle calls –

and the boys are off on their awfully big adventure.
She learns a new geography –
Rommel and Desert Rats,
Sidi Rezegh.

and the last post.

Six long years and the train pulls in;
she searches the confusion of shouts and smoke
and then –
only her older brother appears
through the steam.

The Girl from Qumbu

Thatched huts on the hills
the eyes of speckled cattle;
these are the shapes of her childhood –
the girl from Qumbu.

A cowry – it is a darning shell,
it is an ear –
she hears the ocean,
the whispering voices of her grandmothers.

The crack on its underside –
this is where we come into the world –
from the salty sea inside –
the white circles milk makes,
the white enamel bucket.

This brown and spotted shell
the hides of Nguni cows,
the headlamps of her dad's Humber
the shade of the amber tree –

like a tadpole finds its way out –
she breaks open.

Tsitsa Falls

She's come here to this place;
one could say nothing has changed –
the river spirals around the hills
decade after decade,
the reflections twist and twirl –
her brothers jumping daredevils,
the rafts they made –
branches from floods,
rope and wire and old car tyres.
Neil, his fair hair glinting.

When she heard of his death
there was no air to breathe.
she took her bicycle and rode to the river –
to the bright sun,
a pool of concentric circles.

The other raft
on the sea amid bombs
Neil clinging to the flotsam
in the oily, cold sea.

Now she's here again at Tsitsa Falls –
the river empty of boys,
empty of rafts and ropes –
only a coucal calls;
the waters eddy
round and round.

The day I wore yellow

She died and I wore yellow
and white polka dots;
they danced before my eyes
made me mad,
dizzy in the sun,
wheeling a cart wheel,
I spun around
on the grass I watched the sky;
of course I didn't know
how to make it stop.

She made a promise
from the clouds;
I could look up and see her.
She'd write messages
even when it was windy up there.
I looked into her blue eyes –
I knew she'd keep hers –
so I made mine.

The day she died

Tonight, as I walk, midnight swallows me
on a road only I can see.
Night blades
its way to my tongue –
a dance that tastes like old tin.
Midnight swallows me tonight –
the last of the road spits me into morning.
The day ends even as I say it,
the day that doesn't know.
The slice of light that tears the sky,
this morning should be banished,
be hounded to a black hole.
The world should know yesterday
ended.

Papa

I carried a pebble
in my pocket —
a keepsake for you.

My word, a small grain,
a granule in my hand.
Language and rhymes were
a way to sustain you.

It was a long voyage —
my breath the tides
looking for you
down a dead-end street —
a mere eye,
eyes looking past.

I thought I heard
a quiet laugh
but it was just an echo
of emptiness.

You never found me —
the place
or the moment
like a wave.

A Diet of Worms

High school was a time of worms
not Blake's invisible worm – I didn't know that then.
I knew Oupa dug worms and kept them in a can
for fishing. I knew Momma opened a can of worms
wanting me to go St Mary's in Jo'burg,
but Papa said the government school was good enough.
After the holidays we took the long road back
from the seaside, stopped for petrol and a Cadbury's Lunch Bar.
It was stale – and I then saw it –
a tiny worm wriggling. I had missed it on my first bite.

I learned of Luther and The Diet of Worms,
black people ate fried mopane worms and Papa called me
'a book-worm'. In biology we dissected earthworms,
learned about measly pork and tape worms.
Then in Standard 7 a worm got into Tsafendas and told him to kill
the Prime Minister. It changed the country's history.
It changed my history.
Within months a worm activated Papa's head –
a worm he silenced with a gunshot.

If we'd left the seaside early and not stopped,
if I had gone to St Mary's and not to Milner High
on the red dusty veld, Papa would have sat under the pin-oak
missing me, and planning our holidays to the bushveld
and, when the worm spoke to Tsafendas,
Papa would have shaken his head and his own worm
would have fallen out of his ear.

Sterkfontein Bones

The cave holds the bones
the cave and also the hospital
Sterkfontein, dust as old as stone.
She wondered if it had changed,
if there was concrete or
wooden walkways, a shop
that sold resin skulls for lamps.

The narrow opening still
concealed by kiepersol and wild olive,
she saw the bright bones –
a toe and a tooth.
It's called The Cradle now
but it's really a trapdoor –
animals fell in to die
on a heap of bones.

The other Sterkfontein
they called Groendakkies;
she sat with him on a bench there
under yellow apples of a syringa tree.
What men don't understand, they
call madness,
she'd read it somewhere.
He wanted her to pick up the apples
that had fallen;
the silver apples of the moon
the golden apples of the sun,
but she would not.
Even if she did
she'd only have bones –
a tooth and a toe.

Sabotage

10 February 1968

Now softly – through his mouth –
the simple breath that kept him alive,
his chest moving up and down.
She watched him, never seen him weak or sick.
It frightened her – more than the bandaged head,
the passive body under the hospital covers,
unable to take charge or know the answers.
He had known all the answers –
so had she then at sixteen. She had been full of answers,
she his favourite, his golden girl.
And now there were no answers.
His heart and lungs moving mechanically; he could be sleeping.
She'd never watched him sleep – he was always awake,
ready for the next thing – his mind quick and flashing.
And now his brain – rigged with explosives, the fuse lit –
was blown out like a sabotaged station.
And now here he lay – blasted away by his own hand,
the fort of her life, the main supply.

questions of the night

my

sleep

takes me,

filled with stars,

into a dark night.

and I drift in a little boat

all alone. In the distance, I see a light rising;

the gleam of a gold-burnished moon. And, in the silence all around, the glass-still ocean,

and then the phone rings and breaks the night and with it my mind and my heart like a little bird. It is a stranger's voice – a voice I ought to know.

Who wakes me from a dream of stars? Can it be the voice of God or is it you Father? A question suited to the night. I stand naked, cold. Why do you call and why now when I am sixty? Where were you when I was sixteen?

Nefertiti Round

poem for a blue crown

I'm standing on the east bank
of the river Nile searching
for a queen –
a goddess of pyramids.

In the beginning she was
Akhenaten's queen
centred around the sun
then banished
to a northern place.

The walls are broken now
and she dances out of death –
the beautiful one is come but
there are holes –

her face is smashed
her chest gapes
her heart is stolen
twice her ears are pierced
she's lost her crown.

One can see her forehead
once held a heavy crown
one can assemble a complete picture

but let her sit up
and tell us who she is.

Red Poem

Here a red poem
a red desert
a hot sand poem
a red and banished poem

to a queen
who lost her heart
and her head
a blue crowned head.

A queen plagued
by shadows
forces I dare not speak.

A red poem
a red oxide poem
for a blue queen.

Museum in Berlin

In Berlin
there is a glass sarcophagus
where they keep the
head of Nefertiti.
'My Nefertiti,'
my father called her.
In the museum in Berlin
her face is tanned,
her eyelids painted
dark kohl almonds,
her lips stained with
pomegranate,
her necklace a sickle of beads;
coral, ivory and gold,
but her crown is blue
blue lapis lazuli
and tall.

poem for a white girl

In 1962 my father bought
a bust of Nefertiti;
fine white porcelain
from Sheppard and Barker
in Johannesburg.
He placed her on a pedestal
in our lounge
and said she was
the most beautiful woman
in the world.
He said I was like her, that I
was his Nefertiti.
Beautiful women come and go
to his surgery;
they want him to say they
are his Nefertiti.

Now the bust is knocked down
and lies broken in a box
four large pieces
and one small chip.

On the Discovery channel
I watch an archaeologist
open her tomb;
a light falls on a long neck,
her head is bald,
there is an indentation
where a crown once sat,
two holes pierce each ear,
the neck a swan;
the collarbones straight wings,
but her chest is smashed;
a hole gapes.

Desert Heart

A heart lies
in sand,
the ochre wind
whines through
the hollow chambers,
at night a north
wind finds its
way into a
ventricle and
lays eggs into
the velvet wall.

poem for a blue mother

I find your ring after all the years,
I serve tea on a blue altar –
your cross-stitch tablecloth,
your Royal Albert tea set –
patterned winsome,
Five Roses and the silver tray;
the household gods.

Today, when I stopped
at the traffic lights,
the vendor was selling
key rings made of wire;
beaded chillies, ladybirds and
sunflowers.
I bought a heart
– lightweight –
a wire heart beaded with red.

Kalahari heart

The heart of my desert
is a kameeldoring tree
with grey seed pods
like the velvet grey
of rabbit ears. They
fall to the ground
in long listening
for rain.

The heart longs for rain long after ears stop
listening, the heart hears the thunder.

Why we need darkness

Sometimes my world caves in
and I am trapped by landslides
that bury my wide afternoons.
I remember how
the San knew caves
and the dark –
their first singing
put the stars

in the sky.

There is something about
darkness –
the miners

eclipsed in the black earth

for 69 days make me remember
days in the dark
in the belly of the earth.

I sing

songs to the granite sky
to stay sane
until rescuers

punch a hole into the rocky roof.
I forget that I need darkness,
to be buried alive
in a dark chamber – waiting,
recording the oxygen I use,
days,

anthems to put the stars

back.

Ash of Fire

The wind changed direction in the night.
When I wake, a fine dusting of black ash.
I stoop to wipe it, but it smears the floor.
The remains of twenty thousand hectares of fynbos;
proteas, restios, ericas,
the ash of snakes,
buck and birds.
It blows through the window, fills the air.
I breathe them through the day;
at night they become part of me.

On the beach the ash –
a filigree too fine to hold –
little papers, they crumble,
smear my hand.
I make ash drawings
to remember them by.
The mountainside, the blackened seed heads,
the charred out bones, skeletons of bird and bush,
trees and tortoises;
a death yard, but also – hard to say this –
a yard of nutrients.

After the Fires

We take a drive to Stanford;
on both sides of the road
the bush is charred and black,
a pall of smoke hangs over the lagoon,
smouldering mounds mark the mountain side
like a black and white photograph,
only it's not a photograph.
The fire is still waiting
under charred piles,
waiting for a wind to whip it up.
We stop at a farm gate –
the springs melded to the post –
the road is a bleak white belt,
the burnished sign to Crystal Kloof –
the proteas are sooty candelabras – dark cups;
yesterday they held soft pink torches.
A farm building, an ochre rectangle like an altered photograph.
On the lagoon's side a fisherman's cottage,
alone amongst the black stems of burnt wattle,
its thatched roof still intact
and then I see it – there on the telephone wire –
a bird –
its feathers fuming – smoke signals to the wind.

Old Year

You keep telling yourself to suck moisture from the year,
take it into your mouth even if it tastes of aloe.
Suck it through the smoke, through the burnt trees.
The images of your family, the photographs that hang,
charred skeletons, framed in old gold.
They hover like ghosts, speckled and spotted, telling you
you too will die.
A family tree arranged like now – fence posts –
the shared genes, stories gather on your skin;
they smell of smoke, black and ash. Over your shoulder
you see feathers smouldering.

I was old when I began – a fracture of hope –
I didn't know how to find, in the pitch dark,
sweet memories. They are rendered to ash.
I stoop to take the day.

Now you're outside – the veld stretches –
it is the middle of the night and you enter the sides –
your mother's side – the Nguni cows lie on sand,
where silver holds cowry shells.
Your father's side feels like a little river lost and broken.
and you are walking in a mirror
through acres of scrub, yellow tainted and unscathed
though fire licks, and you think you should spit at it – at their
lives.
The time you have is yours, not theirs. You did not inherit much
more than mist –
and, in tiny rivulets, it runs down your cheeks.
You know this; it is a hard thing to die,
but being alone in the rain on white sand
is all you need.

Morning Gifts

Call me to the river –
a young girl covered in a white cloth
before the light parts the night from the dark lagoon.
Call me to come – clap, clap –
bowing low, humble, to ask
for permission to wake you
to raise you from your sleep.
Call me to bring gifts
Black Label beer,
snuff and Five Roses.
Call me to the water still
like the air, then let a breeze breathe
across my shoulders as
I pull the white shawl closer.
Call me to cup my hands
to clap one, two, three.
Call me to greet you mother and grandmothers
and I will breathe in a mouthful
of beer and spit it out onto the sand,
out and out I pour
the three bottles from my mouth –
the foam –
Call me to kneel on the sand next to the water where
I've poured the beer, sprinkled the snuff
and the tea,
bringing you my requests.

A heron swoops in,
he stands one-legged waiting for a fish to stir
I don't think he's seen me.

La Bourdique

The ceiling of the room is faded blue.
A large rusty hook is nailed
into the beam from which the farmer, long ago,
hung his smoked sausages and hams.
The room I am writing in is old,
outside the window pear trees
are so gnarled blossoms push
hard for spring.
Beyond them the nearest hills float
above the fog.
Early this morning, when I was still
in bed, a swallow flew into
the room, circled, saw its error,
and escaped again,
alighted on a beam
of the old barn.
Down beyond the garden is a field,
lucerne is ten inches high.
On the corner of the road, the Madonna
stands, her hands outstretched,
her veil blue.
Her back turned to me.

Hiding like a Huguenot

TO ANDRE' GAUCH – Huguenot Blacksmith and Farmer fled the Languedoc, France, arrived in South Africa on the ship Spierdyk in 1690.

Like a Huguenot, I hide
in the Noir forests of the
Languedoc. I am
holed up for a
month in Martrin.
Winter reluctantly withdraws
mists snake up valleys.
The pear trees withhold
white blossoms for a few more weeks.
I walk the road to Coupiac,
along the pathways of Knights Templars
and Albigensian crusaders.
I confess my thoughts to pissenlit
along the way, sigh
longings to yellow forsythia.
Chestnut groves are bare.
I cannot hide,
not even when a dust devil
sweeps across the red lands,
torments, dances
in the road.
I can only hear it. Will it pick me up
and cast me headlong down the
cliffside?
An old woman passes, hides her face in her coat,
she won't look at me.
I am tired of hiding in this rocky
land, walking steep hills and cold.
I long to drive away to Carcasonne,
to the night cafes
listen to music, sing
and dance and maybe
see the eye of a man.
He is looking at me
and I am smiling back
at him.

Four Voices of Marriage

Paper:
the voice of blue
things not spoken.
I lost something
long ago in the desert.
For forty years
it lay hidden,
a diamond in the dust.
A flash flood carried it far.

China:
the voice of union,
here the darkness is
broken by trees.
I know the secret,
see it in a stranger's eyes
watch it in the reflection of shop windows.

Silver:
the voice of frozen lakes.
I'm trapped in ice,
the memory of sun seeps
from my heart.
A fossil recalls
a dream I once had.
I used to believe in fairies.

Ruby:
is the colour of blood
bloodlines,
the lines of connection
umbilical cords,
your body parts and mine
birth, our children
our lives

Maps of Memory

The world is written on paper as if it is stone;
ink wraps it – a woollen ball, a spider's web.
Marked are the lines – where to, which way, a witch's way;
the atlas maps out deserts, jungles, a city,
even the heavens are charted,
the stars pin pointed, pricked as on canvas.

I live on ley lines – watch planets rise before dawn,
the sun rise at summer solstice,
the moon in winter –
from the Hottentot's Holland to the neck of Constantiaberg,
the elephant watches, her eye a grotto. A line links
the cave on the Kalk Bay mountain to Hangklip.
I join the dots, read the markings like letters;
these engravings and graphs
map my world in invisible ink.
I trace the threads, the paths lead me back;
memory like hieroglyphs
scratched in sand, paper, stone.
I follow the contours back to childhood –
the tiny ivory elephant in a malachite box,
I trace a crystal enclosed in a gold cage, a little lamp;
the threads mark my place in the world,
lines like letters, scorings in sand and stone
connect me to a doll's tea set,
to the words in my mother's childhood book.

Marriage

Not wanting it –
I stay for 42 years …

Held inside an eye – I am helpless,
unable to say yes or no –
with my hands I feel the walls
of the red cavern.

Sun breaks
the seam of night and day –
morning.

hoping for birds

Hoping for birds
all I heard –
the sound of a few drops of rain;
I wouldn't have known
the little yellow leaf was dancing –
not from its own joy,
but from drops, like bullets
and I remembered the story
of the policemen's game;
how they sat around a fire
and told the prisoner to sing.
He didn't have a good voice
so they shot at his feet
and he danced
light and nimble.
They laughed as the brandy flowed
and shots strayed into the night,
the one with the gun forgetting,
sitting back to stare at the dark
every now and then a pot-shot at a star.
The dancer, his legs sharp streaks of lightning
pinning him to the ground,
afraid the policemen would wake;
a dark statue he stood
as the embers died,
then edged himself towards the thorn trees,
melding himself into their forms –
hoping to be a bird.

The story of how I love a river

This is the story of how I love a river –
how I float on gold-brown water
to the open mouth of the sea rippling brown,
water from far flowing
glows like glass,
sand sifted gold,
how I plunge my body,
allow it to turn and be carried headlong
or spin around,
watch my feet lead me to the sea,
how cold blue water meets warm brown,
waves running, and the incoming tide
swirl and eddy.
How the rocks, sand dug away,
create rapids.
how I lie long and flat – how terns on the bank lift
how, like all my worries,
they are bits of torn paper
swirling up and away.

Old Photographs in a Junk Shop

A girl and her dog,
a boy with his ball,
a young woman at the docks waving to a ship,
a soldier in uniform –
I sort through old sepia photographs –
in cabinets marked men, women, children, groups –
cameos of mothers, babies, young couples, street photographs,
family groups, weddings.

The lost ones, the broken ones
torn and tattered
abandoned –
after death, divorce
the damaged ones,
discarded ones, given away
to charity shops, junk shops,
the dump.
I take them and look –
the images remind me of graves –
each a headstone.

This woman has brown eyes, a shy smile, a heart-shaped face.
This man is a soldier, this one a sailor.
Here is a boy in a sailor suit, a girl in a tartan skirt holding a cat
her face is plump, her cheeks dimpled.
Did she lose weight and become pretty?
Was she loved?
This man could be 100 years old –
what could his life tell?
I want to frame them and place them on the wall
with my family.

Look at this young woman – her neck an elegant curve,
her skin clear, her nose finely chiselled –
she could be my mother's sister – the one she never had.
I can create a new life

in a word narrative, a painting —
I could collage and draw in the missing pieces.
I gaze at the discarded lives and
think of wars, holocausts, migrations —
these photographs like bodies
lying in boxes,
I can raise them up again.

the Longitude of Water

I'm learning to die
      to lose the world;
its map of waterlessness,
      a primitive picture
like the elephant, skin of baobab
      is a chart of wisdom,
a longitude of longing,
      it's my heart that counts
blindly, without words;
      a dictionary of memory.

The elephant I write –
in a craze of drought, wood and metal
is a route to laughter.
I walk a long time to a beach and
find a scallop.
It glows silver, a misty welcome
above the peaks of Maanskynkop,
across the Kleinriver lagoon.
I see a shooting star, hear a Mozart clarinet
then silence.

My words seek out a new place

the black spot at the
centre.

equinox caller

And it was a day – the searing heat,
the super perigee moon
orange through the smoke of fynbos fires
across the bay.
I was making tea and you came and called me,
so I left the tea
and went down into the garden to meet
the visitor
but he had disappeared and we were afraid.
The man came on a motorbike,
his rucksack and girlfriend on the back and
we pointed to the path – and a nearby bush –
dry and longing for water.
He pulled the bush and it came away easily
– and there it was –
the snake – coiled, gold flecked darkness –
a burnished head, eyes staring. A puff-adder,
the snake man said
a mature male, about three years old;
so that's how I know to say 'he'.
The snake man lifted him with a prong;
the snake did not protest, he simply allowed it,
his thick slackness heavy, suspended for a moment.
He seemed embarrassed;
it was an undignified pose for one so regal
and he slipped into the container,
hiding his head.
The man and his girl and our equinox guest left for Silvermine
and we stood and stared at the dark place
where the bush had been.
There was something about his vulnerability
and I felt like the poet – that I'd been in the presence of a king.

The tea was cold and I did not make more.
We stood on the veranda instead and waited
for the perigee moon – burnished like his head –
to rise.

found poem

(*Weight*, Jeanette Winterson)

In the beginning – nothing
not even space and time.
You could have thrown the universe at me
And I would have caught it in one hand.
a strange time –
what I know is told to me
in radioactive whispers;
that's all there is left –
a great shout into silence.

What is it that you contain?
the dead
time
light
patterns of millennia opening in your gut.
Every minute, in each of you,
a few million potassium atoms
succumb to radioactive decay.

These tiny atomic events
locked inside ever since;
a star-sized bomb exploded
nothing into being –

your first parent was a star.

the bush at sunrise

The black and burnish of the bush at sunrise
like gold leaf on an ancient icon,
the mish-mash of twigs and stems.
I see faces and bodies in the chaos,
like gold leaf on an ancient icon;
patterns of green and mauve, black and brown.
I see faces and bodies in the chaos,
life celebrating itself,
patterns of green and mauve, black and brown;
a spring cuckoo calling for its mate;
life celebrating itself
what have they to say after all these years?
a spring cuckoo calling for its mate,
the mish-mash of twigs and stems.
what have they to say after all these years
the black and burnish of the bush at sunrise?

South Easter

They say a gale force wind
is tumbling Devil's Peak today,
a great sea is making its way
against the grey sky of the elephant,
Hottentots' Holland
and Helderberg jagger the edges.
They say the wind releases
an old bird with straw hair;
bewitched, it blows and batters
its way to the waterfall.
A rock pigeon is beaten into
the rusty-red cliffs but,
they say, canaries can find
each other even in this wind.

red dress

your breath in my neck

I try to picture nine naked fish
quicksilver in motion
utter answers to the sun

I'm a bird
caught in a void
– stretch my ear

thick between pearl breasts
a genial finger wakes me
red dress –
caught breathless.

on hearing my friend is to emigrate

Rooted here
here on this summer's day
this South Africa
this Cape
when in spring
I am seduced
by green wheat fields
the purple haze across
the lagoon
herons flying low
and in autumn the
pear trees and apples
of Elgin
golden poplars
alongside the N2
soon to be sucked bare by
the northwest wind.

Rooted here
by purple mountains –
the Helder and the Hottentot
hold me. In winter
I want to fly
high over the Hex
gaze at the lair
of leopards
where the snow hides
on the cold side.

Rooted here
this Cape
this South Africa
I cannot leave even
as loud-mouthed politicians
sound alarms
and sirens shriek

or when I see a child
on the side of the road
a dog so thin its skeleton
walks as if by itself
its eyes hollow
tortoises of
despair.
I am rooted here
a cedar
a yellowwood
a protea.

myth of myself

A man took me away –
I tried to cling
but a fish sucked my skin and opened me
to a decade of convulsions –
I climbed in and out of Chinese boxes,
met a woman with fire eyes –
she gave me a key, a way out,
although she was lost herself.
Every step of the way was a continental shift –
leaving my mother, the myth of myself,
that perhaps I could be happy
under the influence of men.
But then I burst into the wilderness –
hiked across stony paths, slept under stars,
I spent weekends in heather, on high cliffs.
The path took me close to the sea –
there I found a sand dollar,
perhaps it was the currency of love –
but I could buy only a skeleton.
The years washed away – I thought I was happy –
that I'd saved the sky
under my tent's blue canopy.

Remembering Promises

There is a prayer that changes the world
but I can't remember it.
I pick up five stones –
Soweto, Khayelitsha, Sharpeville, Boipatong, Blikkiesdorp.

God knows the grass is green here,
that trees have a secret life;
only those willing to climb to the top
will hear their whisper.
What do you think when people promised houses
still live in shanties?

The sound of water is what I think.

The prayer of five stones –
Soweto, Khayelitsha, Sharpeville, Boipatong, Blikkiesdorp;
there is a prayer that changes the world,
I can't remember it.
The sound of water is what I think.

House at Kolmanskop

Everybody's gone;
those who once lived here,
who occupied my flesh,
and I am left with bits of charcoal,
the burnt out fires, the empty grates.
But I pick up a piece and draw
my life – a city of stones –
submerged in sand, it rises.
I'm walking on skin
the colour of a dried out lake,
yet there are acacias near the edge,
but I'm not allowed to call them
acacias anymore;
Australia owns them
and the ones who fled in fear
and the children,
but I stayed
like the dead heads of the cannas,
the agapanthus drying in the garden
dropping black seeds.
The one who desired, who inserted himself,
no longer sees me,
the weight of a cathedral
he no longer worships.
Stained glass and sand bags,
the wine's evaporated,
the red stains, the breadcrumbs
abandoned at Kolmanskop
so I spend days walking sands,
and I occupy my body
with these words.

Zwaanswyk Morning

It is early in the morning –
dark, and the lights
from the city and the embers
glow in the forest
the night jar calls 'Good Lord deliver them' –
we need to listen to that bird.
The firemen have kept vigil all night;
I see the red lights of their fire trucks,
the long low pall of smoke
still hangs over the lower forest,
the small remnant of yesterday's fire.
I watched until after midnight
the flashing lights, and this morning,
I sit outside
on a bench and listen to the dawn birds –
a Cape Robin alights on a branch;
the sky is beginning to lighten
above the Hottentots Holland,
planes are already taking off at the airport,
over du Toit's Kloof the lights
of an incoming plane rising like a star.

Versions of some poems have been published in the following journals and publications: *New Contrast, New Coin, The Cambridge Conference of Contemporary Poetry Review, A Hudson Review, EU Sol Plaatje Poetry Anthologies 2011 – 2014*, and online in: *Incwadi, Deep Water Literary Journal, scrutiny2 – issues in English Studies in Southern Africa*.

Intertextuality:
p19 Sterkfontein Bones – *the silver apples of the moon, the golden apples of the sun* is a reference to Yeats's The Song of the Wandering Aengus
p39 The Story of How I Love a River – the title is a nod to Ted Hugh's poem *Arethusa*; 'Tales from Ovid', Faber and Faber 1997
p43 Found Poem – *Weight*, Jeanette Winterson, Canongate Books, 2006

Thank you to Finuala Dowling for editorial comments on the manuscript and for her poetry workshops.

Thanks to Colleen Higgs for incarnating the rain queen, and who, since 1997, has played an important part in my writing.

Thanks to Anne Schuster for being the most inspiring person.

Thank you to Ron for everything else.

Other Poetry titles by Modjaji Books

The Turtle Dove told Me *by Thandi Sliepen*
Beyond the Delivery Room *by Khadija Heeger*
The Reckless Sleeper *by Haidee Kruger*
Bare & Breaking *by Karin Schimke*
At least the Duck Survived *by Margaret Clough*
removing *by Melissa Butler*
Difficult Gifts *by Dawn Garisch*
Woman Unfolding *by Jenna Mervis*
The Everyday Wife *by Phillippa Yaa de Villiers*
missing *by Beverly Rycroft*
These are the lies I told you *by Kerry Hammerton*
Conduit *by Sarah Frost*
The Suitable Girl *by Michelle McGrane*
Piece Work *by Ingrid Andersen*
Fourth Child *by Megan Hall*
Life in Translation *by Azila Talit Reisenberger*
Please, Take Photographs *by Sindiwe Magona*
Burnt Offering *by Joan Metelerkamp*
Strange Fruit *by Helen Moffett*
Oleander *by Fiona Zerbst*
The Last to Leave *by Maragret Clough*
Now the world takes these breaths *by Joan Metelerkamp*

www.ingramcontent.com/pod-product-compliance
Lightning Source LLC
Chambersburg PA
CBHW071012160426
43193CB00012B/2024